AF224990

ANOINTED ONES

The Realm and Lifestyle of the Anointed

Raphael Stephen Samuels

Anointed Ones:

The Realm and Lifestyle of the Anointed

Copyright © by Raphael Stephen Samuels 2019

All rights reserved. No portion of this book without permission may be reproduced, stored in a retrieval system, or transmitted in any form or by any means — electronic, photocopy, or recorded, without the written prior consent of the author, as it is strictly prohibited. Excerpts and links may be used, provided that full and clear credit is given to the author with specific direction to the original content.

If you would like to use material from the book for short quotations or occasional page copying for personal or group study, is permitted and encouraged prior written permission must be obtained on request by contacting the publisher at pastorraph45@gmail.com.

Scripture quotations are taken from the NEW INTERNATIONAL VERSION BIBLE (NIV) and NEW KING JAMES VERSION (NKJV)

Email address: pastorraph45@gmail.com

ISBN Number: ISBN 978-1-9160600-2-9

DEDICATION

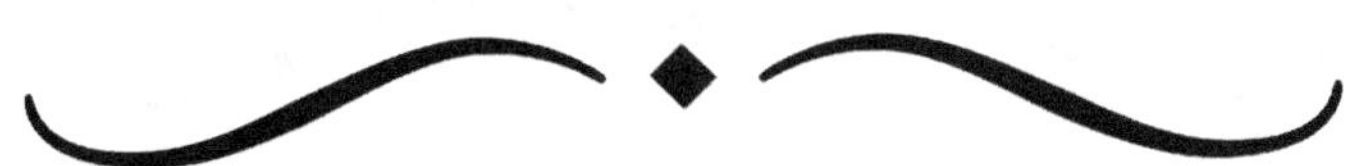

This book is dedicated to my parents and spiritual mentors. To Kwasi Ohene Antwi, my premier spiritual mentor who God used to lay the foundation of the Holy Spirit baptism in my life; thank you for introducing me to the Holy Spirit and setting me up for adventures of the anointed life in the Holy Spirit. I am eternally grateful.

ACKNOWLEDGEMENTS

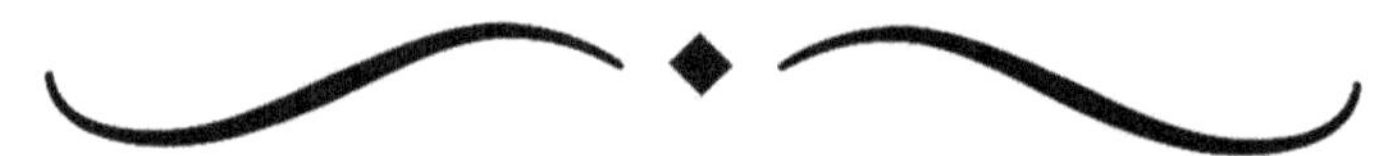

I would like to honour my Heavenly Father, God Almighty for the gift of writing. It is humbling to share my life journey with the world. I would like to give a special thanks to Benjamin Qusi for the opportunity of knowing him as a brother in Christ and a Gospel Minister. He held a conference called the Joshua Troop Conference in April 2019 that really empowered my spirit. It was through the conference that I have been connected to an Author; Esther Jacob who has inspired me to finish and publish this book. I am grateful to you both.

Special thanks to Rev Richard and Rev Ruth Samuels for their loyalty, and to Mercy-Ann and Joshua for their commitment. To Mr Johannes and Vera Zwennes, Jan and Joanna, thanks for your love, encouragement and support. I would also like to thank Prophetess Madaleine Redpath, Evangelist Ellen Damptey, Evangelist Christiana Agyei and Deaconess Lydia Agyei. They have stood with me in the work of the ministry and have been consistent members at Reigners Gospel Church International.

I am grateful to Evangelist Sade Obisesan for her counsel and proofreading the first draft of this book and making valuable contributions. Prophetess Henritta Debrah and my godson, Kelvin Debrah; thanks to you both for being a source of strength and encouragement to me. To Mr Duah and Evangelist Gifty Brobbey family in France, I would like to thank you for your heartfelt love, prayers and giving me the privilege to serve you in the work of the ministry.

To Evangelist Esther Koranteng and family in Belgium; thanks for your encouragement, kindness and support. To Evangelist Joyce Tandoh and Mr Peter Archer, I am grateful for your friendship, counsel and support. I would finally like to thank all members of Reigners Gospel Church International, my fellow ministers and everyone that has contributed to my life especially in this journey of publishing my first book. May God richly bless you.

TABLE OF CONTENTS

INTRODUCTION

Whether you know it or not, each of us is influenced by a spirit beyond ourselves. This book is about how I was introduced to the Holy Spirit; how He empowers and influences my life daily and how He can empower and influence your life to live victoriously and courageously.

God anointed Jesus Christ with the Holy Spirit and power (Acts 10:38). Likewise, Jesus also anoints those who believe in Him with the Holy Spirit and (power) fire (Luke 3:16).

Chapter 1 captures the Genesis of how the Holy Spirit encountered me; how I heard the Gospel of Christ, experienced supernatural rebirth and baptism with the Holy Spirit.

Chapter 2 explores the four kinds of anointed ones:

(1) The Non-Anointed

(2) The Anointed

(3) The Self-Anointed

(4) The Disobedient Anointed

Chapters 3 outlines the personality of the Holy Spirit in the New Testament.

Chapter 4 enumerates the requirements that one needs to satisfy to become an Anointed one.

Chapter 5 deals with persons designated as Anointed ones in the Holy scriptures.

In Chapters 6 and 7 special emphasis is given to the revelation of Jesus as the ultimate Anointed One. Jesus was conceived, born, baptized, anointed, led, empowered and resurrected by the Holy Spirit for our justification, redemption and salvation.

Anointed Ones have attitudes to manifest, responsibilities to discharge, privileges and blessings to enjoy. These are discussed in chapters 8 to 11.

In Chapter 12, I use the parts of the body as an analogy to illustrate how being anointed empowers us to exert Godly influence.

CHAPTER 1
A PERSONAL TOUCH

I first heard the Gospel message of Salvation at the age of 14 in the summer of 1987. My friend Deborah invited me to a Christian youth camp meeting for students on vacation. We made our way and sat in the middle row inside the hall. The hall was packed, and the preacher outlined a profound Gospel message. He talked about the sinfulness of man and the utter helplessness to be saved from deserved wrath, judgement and condemnation of a Holy and righteous God.

He made it clear that God was also a merciful and loving Father who gave His only son, Jesus Christ to pay the death penalty for our sins and redeem all mankind from death to eternal life. I was hearing all this for the first time.

He shouted *"you have a choice to make; today is the day to decide! You need to admit that you are a sinner in need of God's love and forgiveness and have a change of heart from sinful living".* *He told us to believe in Jesus who is sinless and died for all of us. He was buried and resurrected for our Salvation from sin and death to heaven and eternal life.*

He continued; *"if you reject Jesus Christ and God's olive branch of love, you will end up in eternal death. The choice is yours!"*

He paused as to give the congregation a chance to reflect; silence filled the room. My heart began to beat faster. I was at a crossroads of a life changing decision; heaven or hell? Eternal life or eternal death? God's love or God's wrath?

I knew I was living a sinful life of youthful sexual lusts and the anger which caused me to be suspended in primary school. When I was young, in anger, I slapped a classmate of mine who mocked me with such force that he fell to the ground. In 'old school' punishment fashion, I was severely caned in front of the whole school and suspended for two weeks. It was a humbling experience. I reflected, and it dawned on me that just as my sin attracted physical punishment from my head teacher, likewise sin attracts spiritual punishment from a holy God.

As the room was silent, the preacher shouted, "come to the front if you want to receive Jesus; He will forgive your sins, wash you in His precious blood and give you a brand new heart and spirit – a new life on the inside"

I stood up and went to the front. He led us in a prayer of repentance and acceptance of what Jesus did for all mankind on the cross and was able to confess Him as my personal Lord and Saviour. Afterwards, I felt relieved with joy filling my heart.

Thus, began the Genesis of my new Christian life. After the vacation I went back to my secondary school and made new Christian friends who attended the Christian fellowship called the Scripture Union. For some time as a baby Christian, I struggled with the assurance of my salvation especially when I sinned.

In my mind I thought the remedy was to receive Jesus again. At school any time an invitation was made by a guest preacher, I went forward to accept Jesus. My friends began to ask me, "Raphael how many times will you accept Jesus?" I smiled and replied, "I just want to be sure as I wanted to please my Lord Jesus and also dreaded the thought of eternal death and hell fire".

Graciously, God gave me an insatiable desire to read and memorize the Bible. One day as I was reading the book of Hebrews I got to Hebrews 2:9, which reads *"But we do see Jesus who was made lower than the angels for a little while, now crowned with Glory and honour because He suffered death, so that by the Grace of God He might taste death for everyone"*

Jesus tasted death for everyone. I received illumination from this scripture that made me not respond to calls accepting Jesus repeatedly because I knew I was already saved since I believed. I understood that once I had acknowledged and renounced my sins and accepted Jesus' sacrifice on the cross, I don't need to doubt. That settled it for me. I was no more unsure of my salvation. I was fully persuaded and assured that I was saved.

Continuing my Christian journey, I was introduced to someone who was filled with the Holy Spirit; a Christian brother called Kwasi Antwi. He asked me whether I have been baptized with the Holy Spirit. I answered, "I guess not as I didn't hear about the Holy Spirit". I informed him that I have accepted Jesus Christ as my Lord and personal Saviour.

Brother Kwasi explained that I need to receive the Holy Spirit. He referred me to Acts 19: 1-7 where Apostle Paul asked the Ephesian believers:

'Did you receive the Holy Spirit when you believed? So, they said to him, we have not so much heard whether there is a Holy Spirit'. (Acts 19:2, NKJV)

Like these Ephesians, even though I had heard the gospel, repented, received forgiveness of my sins and accepted Christ Jesus, I didn't hear whether there was a Holy Spirit. Brother Kwasi said "Raphael, you need the experience of being baptized with the Holy Spirit".

He said it will open a new realm of the reality of the person, presence and ministry of the Holy Spirit as my

Teacher, Guide, Counsellor, Prayer Partner and Comforter on my Christian journey.

I (John speaking) indeed baptize you with water unto repentance...but Jesus who is coming after me, He will baptize you with the Holy Spirit and fire (power) (Matthew 3:11, NKJV).

Kwasi said this is a realm and life of power available in the Holy Spirit – a life of developing and growing in the gifts and fruit of the Holy Spirit; a dimension of not only praying with my mind but more importantly, praying with my born-again spirit, that is, an unlearned language called *speaking in tongues.*

This makes one speak unknown mysteries to God in prayer with his spirit by the influence of the Holy Spirit. *For if I pray in a tongue, my spirit prays, but my mind is unfruitful. So, what shall I do? I will pray with my spirit, but I will also pray with my understanding; I will sing with my spirit and I will also sing with my understanding* (1 Corinthians 14:14-15).

With all these insights and exhortations, Brother Kwasi was able to create a spiritual thirst and hunger in my heart for the person and presence of the Holy Spirit; His ministry of power, gifts and character development to the believer in Christ.

Brother Kwasi arranged a time of prayer with a few Holy Spirit filled Christians so that I may be baptized with the Holy Spirit. This happened in the summer of 1988 a year after I had been saved. On that day we gathered at our prayer venue in the woods nearby in our secondary school.

We sang and worshipped with some scriptures. Brother Kwasi reminded me to receive by Grace through faith the baptism of the Holy Spirit just as I had received by Grace through faith, salvation through the death, burial and resurrection of Jesus Christ. As we worshipped, Brother Kwasi laid his hands on my head and prayed for me. That was when I realised, I was suddenly overwhelmed with the power and presence of the Holy Spirit that I could not stand on my feet and fell to the ground.

I began to cry tears of joy, then uttered words of praise and thanksgiving to God. I began to utter in prayer words I hadn't learnt – an unknown tongue. I reverted to pray in English interceding for the salvation of my family members and loved ones. The amazing experience was that those I interceded for all came to faith in Christ over a short period of time.

Brother Kwasi reminded me to prayerfully desire spiritual gifts and allow the Holy Spirit to operate through me His gifts according to His will.

Follow the way of love and eagerly desire spiritual gifts, especially the gift of prophesy (1 Corinthians 14:1).

1 Corinthians 12:7-11 ***"Now to each one the manifestation of the Spirit is given for the common good. To one there is given through time Spirit a message of wisdom, to another a message of knowledge by the means of the same Spirit, to another Faith by the same Spirit, to another gifts of healing by that one Spirit, to another miraculous powers, to another prophecy, to another distinguishing between spirits, to another speaking in different kinds of tongues, and to still another the interpretation of tongues, all these are the work of one and the same Spirit, and he distributes them to each one, just as he determines"***.

I desired the gifts of tongues, interpretation of tongues, prophesy, the word of knowledge and healing. By the inspiration of the Holy Spirit I started to pray for the sick to be healed, giving words of knowledge and prophesying in prayer meetings for exhortation, edification and comfort. My Christian life became more adventurous and impactful.

I have experienced and entered the *'Anointed'* realm of the Holy Spirit. Thus, not only was I born of the Spirit but baptized with the Spirit as well. I became bold to witness to others about Jesus; I preached my first sermon and now had the strength to resist my youthful sexual lusts. The spirit of anger and unforgiveness left my soul and I developed patience and forgiveness.

The power of the Holy Spirit has impacted and empowered my soul. It has given me new Holy desires of fervent prayer, studying the Bible, Holy living, and being able to share my faith with conviction and boldness. I have been baptized with the Holy Spirit and anointed for good works for the Kingdom of God.

CHAPTER 2
KINDS OF ANOINTED ONES

There are four kinds of Anointed ones namely:

1) Non-Anointed Ones

2) Anointed Ones

3) Self-Anointed Ones

4) Disobedient Anointed Ones

NON-ANOINTED ONES

Non-anointed Ones are persons who **do not have the Holy Spirit, they also resist His purposes, plans and works.** They are neither Spirit-born nor Spirit-baptized and oppose the agenda and purposes of God. In scriptures they are referred to as children of the Devil or sons of Belial. Examples of non-anointed persons include Pharaoh, Elymas, Herod, Simeon the Sorcerer, Jambres and Jannes.

"These are the people who divide you, who follow mere natural instincts and do not have the Spirit". **(Jude 1:19)**

Non-anointed people do not have the Holy Spirit of God. They are under the influence of the spirits of worldliness, strife and division.

"You, however, are not in the realm of the flesh but are in the realm of the Spirit, if indeed the Spirit of God lives in you. And if anyone does not have the Spirit of Christ, they do not belong to Christ". **(Romans 8:9)**

Non-anointed people are neither Spirit-born nor Spirit-baptized; they do not have the Spirit of Jesus. They have another spirit; the spirit of the devil, the spirit of lies, deception and the spirit of the anti-Christ. Let us explore the nature, character and behaviours of non-anointed ones:

Paul vs Elymas

Elymas the magician was a false prophet who opposed Apostle Paul and Barnabas when they sought to preach Jesus to the proconsul, Sergius Paulus. But Paul filled with the Holy Spirit rebuked Elymas and pronounced temporary blindness on him. This sign of blindness surprised Sergius Paulus who received Paul's teaching about Christ and believed which made him come to the faith in Christ Jesus. Under the Holy Spirit's anointing Paul describes the kind of spirit that was influencing Elymas:

"But Elymas the sorcerer (for that is what his name means) opposed them and tried to turn the proconsul from the faith. Then Saul, who was also called Paul, filled with the Holy Spirit, looked straight at Elymas and said; You are a child of the devil and an enemy of everything that is right! You are full of all kinds of deceit and trickery. Will you never stop perverting the right ways of the Lord? Now the hand of the Lord is against you. You are going to be blind for a time, not even able to see the light of the sun." Immediately mist and darkness came over him, and he groped about, seeking someone to lead him by the hand. When the proconsul saw

what had happened, he believed, for he was amazed at the teaching about the Lord" (Acts 13: 8-12)

A non-anointed one, (Elymas) is described as the following:

- The son of the Devil

- An enemy of all righteousness

- Full of all deceit and villainy

- Perverting the straight ways of the Lord

Beware of persons operating with the spirit of the devil, the spirit of unrighteousness, the spirit of deceit, villainy and the spirit of perversion. This shows they are not anointed and don't have the Spirit of Christ.

Moses vs Jambres and Jannes

God gave Moses a rod to work signs and wonders in Egypt before Pharaoh. When Pharaoh refused to let the Israelites go, Moses put down his rod before Pharaoh and it turned into a snake.

Pharaoh called his magicians, Jambres and Jannes who opposed and challenged Moses by throwing their rods down to turn them to snakes, but they were defeated when Moses' snake swallowed their snakes. Moses then picked up his snake by the tail and it turned back into a rod. In writing to his son Timothy, the Apostle Paul warned him to avoid non-anointed individuals having an appearance of godliness but denying or opposing God's power; He mentioned Jambres and Jannes who opposed Moses as men of corrupt minds who oppose the truth.

"Just as Jannes and Jambres opposed Moses, so also these teachers oppose the truth. They are men of depraved minds, who, as far as the faith is concerned, are rejected. [9] But they will not get very far because, as in the case of those men, their folly will be clear to everyone" (2 Timothy 3: 8-9)

Non-anointed ones (Jannes and Jambres) did not have the Spirit of God. They were:

- Opposed to the truth

- Of corrupt minds

- Disqualified regarding faith in Christ

Peter vs Simon the Sorcerer

Peter arrived in Samaria to pray with the new believers that they might receive the Holy Spirit because they had only been saved and baptized in water in the name of the Lord, but as yet, the Holy Spirit has not fallen on any of them.

...who when they (Peter and John) had come from Samaria, prayed for them (new believers) that they might receive the Holy Spirit. For as yet He had fallen upon none of them. They had only been baptized in the name of the Lord Jesus. Then they laid hands on them, and they received the Holy Spirit. (Acts 8:14-17).

Apostle Peter met Simon a sorcerer (Acts 8: 9-11) who had bewitched the people of Samaria for a long time. Simon the sorcerer pretended to believe in Jesus and was baptized in water too. When he offered Apostle Peter money to buy the power of the Holy Spirit, Peter rebuked him:

"When Simon saw that the Holy Spirit was given at the laying on of the apostles' hands, he offered them money and said, 'Give me also this ability (power) so that everyone on whom I lay my hands may receive the Holy Spirit.'" (Acts 8: 18-19).

Peter answered: "May your money perish with you, because you thought you could buy the gift of God with money! You have no part or share in this ministry, because your heart is not right before God. Repent of this wickedness and pray to the Lord in the hope that he may forgive you for having such a thought in your heart (23) For I see that you are full of bitterness and captive to sin" (Acts 8: 20-23).

It is clear from the above scriptures that Simon was a non-anointed one. He pretended to believe, and his heart was not right before God. He had a hidden agenda to buy the power of the Holy Spirit. Non-anointed ones are unrepentant, have ulterior motives, bound by iniquity, full of wickedness and bitterness. Clearly, the Spirit of God is not residing in such a heart and life. They need to humble themselves, repent, renounce and turn from their wicked ways and put their faith in Jesus for redemption.

"Whoever conceals their sins does not prosper, but the one who confesses and renounces them finds mercy". (Proverbs 28:13).

<u>ANOINTED ONES</u>

Anointed ones are persons born of the Holy Spirit and baptised with the Holy Spirit. They are Spirit-born and Spirit-baptized persons.

*Jesus answered, most assuredly, I say to you, **unless one is born of water and the Spirit, he cannot enter the kingdom of God.** That which is **born of the flesh is flesh, and that which is born of the Spirit is spirit.** Do not marvel that I said to you, **'You must be born again'.** The wind blows where it wishes, and you hear the sound of it, but cannot tell where it comes from and where it goes. **So is everyone who is born of the Spirit.** (John 3:5-8)*

***And because you are sons, God has sent forth the Spirit of His Son into our hearts, crying out, Abba, Father!** (Galatians 4:6)*

They have heard, believed, received the **Gospel of Christ** and the **life of Christ, that is, Eternal life**.

*For God so love the world that he gave His only begotten Son that **whosoever believes in Him** should not perish but have eternal life.* (John 3:16).

I have been crucified with Christ; it is no longer I who live, but Christ lives in me; and the life which I now live in the flesh, I live by faith in the Son of god, who loved me and gave Himself for me. (Galatians 2:20).

Anointed Ones are indwelt and led by the Holy Spirit.

But if the Spirit of Him who raised Jesus from the dead dwells in you, he who raised Christ from the dead will also give life to your mortal bodies through his Spirit who dwells in you. (Romans 8:11).

For as many as are led by the Spirit of God, these are the sons of God. (Romans 8:14).

Our Lord Jesus is the **Chief or ultimate Anointed One**. He was **conceived** by the Holy Spirit (Luke 1:35), **born** of the Holy Spirit (Luke 1:35), **anointed** with the Holy Spirit (Acts

10:38), **filled** and **led** by the Holy Spirit (Luke 4:1), **empowered** by the Holy Spirit (Luke 4:14) and **resurrected** by the Holy Spirit (Romans 8:11) from the dead for our justification and redemption.

In Acts 19:1-7, Apostle Paul found disciples of John the Baptist who believed in Christ but were not baptized or anointed with the Holy Spirit.

"While Apollos was at Corinth, Paul took the road through the interior and arrived at Ephesus. There he found some disciples and asked them, "Did you receive the Holy Spirit when you believed?" They answered, "No, we have not even heard that there is a Holy Spirit." So, Paul asked, "Then what baptism did you receive?" "John's baptism," they replied, Paul said, "John's baptism was a baptism of repentance. He told the people to believe in the one coming after him, that is, in Jesus." On hearing this, they were baptized in the name of the Lord Jesus. When Paul placed his hands on them, the Holy Spirit came on them, and they spoke in tongues and prophesied. There were about twelve men in all" (Acts 19:1-7)

They had only experienced John's baptism of repentance. Apostle Paul preached Christ to them and baptized them in water in the name of the Lord Jesus. He laid his hands on them to be anointed with the Holy Spirit and they spoke in tongues and prophesied. These 12 anointed men became the founding members for the Church of Ephesus. All truly Spirit-born and Spirit-baptized believers in Christ are Anointed Ones.

SELF-ANOINTED ONES

Self-anointed ones are persons who exalt themselves to divine offices or callings without God's anointing, appointment and approval. The book of Hebrews 5:4 warns us that no one should take the honour of spiritual callings, positions or offices by himself but rather one should be called, anointed and appointed by God.

"And no one takes this honour on himself, but he receives it when called by God, just as Aaron was" (Hebrews 5:4)

When King Saul intruded into the priestly office of Samuel, he erred, and it contributed to his dethronement by God from reigning as King over Israel.

You have to prayerfully discover where, when and what you are anointed and appointed for and stay faithful in your calling, ministry or office.

Do not take upon yourself a spiritual calling or office without God's initiation, anointing, ordination or appointment because *there are diversities of gifts but the same Spirit, and there are differences of administrations but the same Lord. There are diversities of operations but the same God which works all in all.* (1 Corinthians 12:4-6 KJV)

Receive the grace right now to discern how God operates uniquely with you to fulfil a ministry that Jesus has called you to, with the gifts of the Holy Spirit given to you.

For the same God who operated in the apostolic ministry of Peter to the Jews also operated uniquely in the apostolic ministry of Paul to the Gentiles. Peter and Paul, were both apostles but God operated in and with each of them differently to reach two different groups.

Avoid the spirit of Absalom (2 Samuel 15:4,10; 2Samuel 18:9-10), the spirit of Adonijah (1 Kings 1:5; 2:25) and the spirit of Korah (Numbers 16:1-5; 26:10-11).

Moreover, Absalom said, "Oh, that I were made a judge in the land, and everyone who has any suit would come to me; then I will give him justice. As soon as you shall hear the sound of the trumpet, then you shall say 'Absalom reigns in Hebron!" (2 Samuel 15:4,10).

Then Absalom met the servants of David. Absalom rode on a mule. The mule went under the thick boughs of a great terebinth tree, and his head got caught in the tree; he was left hanging between heaven and earth (2 Samuel 18:9-10).

1 Kings 1:5, NIV reads: "Now Adonijah, whose mother was Haggith, put himself forward and said, 'I will be king." So, he got chariots and horses ready, with fifty men to run ahead of him".

So, King Solomon sent by the hand of Benaiah the son of Jehoiada, and he struck Adonijah down, and he died (1 Kings 2:25).

Numbers 16: 1-5, NIV reads: "Now Korah, the son of Izhar, the son of Kohath, the son of Levi, and Dathan and Abiram, the sons of Eliab, and On, the son of Peleth, sons of Reuben, took men (2) And they rose up before Moses, with certain of the children of Israel, two hundred and fifty princes of the assembly, famous in the congregation, men of renown (3) And they gathered themselves together against Moses and against Aaron, and said unto them, Ye take too much upon you, seeing all the congregation are holy, every one of them, and the Lord is among them: wherefore then lift ye up yourselves above the congregation of the Lord? (4) And when Moses heard it, he fell upon his face (5) And he spake unto Korah and unto all his company, saying, even tomorrow the Lord will shew who are his, and who is holy; and will cause him to come near unto him: even him whom he hath chosen will he cause to come near unto him"

Numbers 26: 10-11, NIV reads: "The earth opened its mouth and swallowed them along with Korah, whose followers died when the fire devoured the 250 men. And they served as a warning sign (11) The line of Korah, however, did not die out"

These three men died tragically by divine judgment because of their selfish ambition, self-promotion and rebellion. ***Avoid selfish ambition and self-promotion;*** Stay faithful and true to your unique calling, office, mandate, ministry and gifts that God in Christ has graciously given to you.

DISOBEDIENT ANOINTED ONES

Disobedient anointed ones are persons who were anointed by God but fell from grace through their disobedience to God's instructions, words and ways. Examples include Lucifer, King Saul, Samson and King Solomon. When an anointed one becomes disobedient to God and refuses to repent, they fall from the grace and the glory God gave them. We will discuss the following persons:

Lucifer vs Jesus

The first disobedient anointed one is Lucifer also known as *Satan*. He was an Anointed cherub but he fell due to **_pride._**

"You were anointed as a guardian cherub for, so I ordained you. You were on the holy mount of God; you walked among the fiery stones, you were blameless in your ways from the day you were created till wickedness was found in you".
(Ezekiel 28: 14-15)

"He replied, "I saw Satan fall like lightning from heaven"

(Luke 10:18).

Our Lord Jesus, on the other hand, is humble and anointed with the oil of gladness above His fellows because He loved righteousness and hated lawlessness.

"And being found in appearance as a man, he humbled himself by becoming obedient to death— even death on a cross! Therefore, God exalted him to the highest place and gave him the name that is above every name." (Philippians 2: 8-9, NIV)

You have loved righteousness and hated wickedness;

therefore God, your God, has set you above your

companions by anointing you with the oil of joy" (Hebrews

1:9, NIV)

Lucifer fell from grace through disobedience and pride, but Christ was exalted for His humility and love for righteousness.

King Saul vs King David

King Saul was disobedient and unrepentant to God's instructions through Prophet Samuel and received God's judgment by being removed from reigning as King.

"For rebellion is like the sin of divination,

and arrogance like the evil of idolatry.

Because you have rejected the word of the Lord,

he has rejected you as king." (1 Samuel 15:23, NIV)

King David, on the other hand, had been truly repentant in reference to Psalm 51 when he disobeyed God. He committed adultery and killed Uriah, Bathsheba's husband. Because King David sincerely repented of his adultery and murder, God pardoned him from the death penalty but chastised him with the death of the child of the adulterous affair and with the sword of the Ammonites (2 Samuel 12:9-15).

As an Anointed One, despising the word of God has serious consequences.

"And he said to the human race, the fear of the Lord—that is wisdom, and to shun evil is understanding" (Job 28:28, NIV)

"You who fear him, trust in the Lord— He is their help and shield" (Psalm 115:11, NIV)

"Fear the Lord, you his holy people,
for those who fear him lack nothing" (Psalm 34:9, NIV)

It is better to walk in the reverential fear of God which attracts His blessings than to walk in the flesh.

Samson vs Joseph

Joseph refused to sin against God by rejecting his master's wife's offer to commit adultery with him. In due time God vindicated and promoted him to be the second in command ruler of Egypt.

"No one is greater in this house than I am. My master has withheld nothing from me except you, because you are his wife. How then could I do such a wicked thing and sin against God?" (Genesis 39:9, NIV)

Samson was an anointed one, but the Spirit of the Lord left him when he disobeyed God. He broke the Nazarene vow and revealed the secret of his anointing to Delilah, who shaved his hair as he slept on her lap. Samson lost his supernatural strength and was taken captive by his enemies who gouged out his eyes, mocked and afflicted him.

"After putting him to sleep on her lap, she called for someone to shave off the seven braids of his hair, and so began to subdue him. And his strength left him" (Judges 16:19).

Then she called, "Samson, the Philistines are upon you!" He awoke from his sleep and thought, 'I'll go out as before and shake myself free." But he did not know that the Lord had left him (Judges 16:20).

Disobedience is costly. It costed Samson his anointing and eyesight. He became weak and blind through disobedience.

Let us stop sinning and disobeying God; let us be obedient anointed children of God.

As **obedient children***, do not conform to the evil desires you had when you lived in ignorance. But just as he who called you is Holy, so be holy in all you do; for it is written: Be holy because I am holy.* (1 Peter 1:14-16).

For you were once darkness, but now you are light in the Lord. Live as children of light (for the fruit of the light consists in all goodness, righteousness and truth) and find out what pleases the Lord. Have nothing to do with the fruitless deeds of darkness, but rather expose them. It is shameful even to mention what the disobedient do in secret. **(Ephesians 5:8-12)**

What kind of Anointed One are you? Are you an obedient or disobedient anointed one? Are you walking as an obedient anointed child of light?

CHAPTER 3
THE PERSON OF THE ANOINTING

Romans 8:27: "And he who searches our hearts knows the mind of the Spirit, because the Spirit intercedes for God's people in accordance with the will of God"

The Holy Spirit is an invisible person. He is a person who has a will, mind and emotions (Romans 8:27). He can be grieved, lied to, quenched and fellowshipped with. Looking at each book of the New Testament can help reveal the personality, character and work of the Holy Spirit in the life of an anointed person.

In **Matthew**, the Holy Spirit is the **Source of the Messianic conception.**

But as he considered these things, behold, an angel of the Lord appeared to him in a dream, saying, Joseph, son of David, do not fear to take Mary as your wife, for that which is conceived in her is from the Holy Spirit (Matthew 1:20).

In **Mark**, the Holy Spirit is our **Spokesman**.

And when they bring you to trial and deliver you over, do not be anxious beforehand what you are to say, but say whatever is given you in that hour, for it is not you who speak, but the Holy Spirit (Mark 13:11).

In **Luke**, the Holy Spirit is **God's Gift to all who ask for Him.**

If you then, who are evil, know how to give good gifts to your children, how much more will the heavenly Father give the Holy Spirit to those who ask him! (Luke 11:13).

In **John**, the Holy Spirit is the **Spirit of Truth, our Helper, Teacher and Guide.**

But when the Helper comes, whom I will send to you from the Father, the Spirit of Truth, who proceeds from the Father, he will bear witness about me (John 15:26)

When the Spirit of truth comes, he will guide you into all the truth, for he will not speak on his own authority, but whatever he hears he will speak, and he will declare to you the things to come (John 16:13).

In **Acts**, the Holy Spirit is the **Spirit of Power.**

But you shall receive power when the Holy Spirit has come upon you, and you shall be my witnesses in Jerusalem and in all Judea and Samaria, and to the end of the earth (Acts 1:8)

In **Romans**, the Holy Spirit is our **Intercessor and the Spirit of love.**

Likewise, the Spirit helps us in our weakness. For we do not know what to pray for as we ought, but the Spirit himself intercedes for us with groaning too deep for words. And he who searches the heart knows what is the mind of the Spirit, because the Spirit intercedes for the saints according to the will of God (Romans 8:26-27)

And hope does not disappoint because the love of God is poured in our hearts through the Holy Spirit who has been given to us (**Romans 5:5**)

In *1 Corinthians*, the Holy Spirit is the **Spirit of Power, Wisdom, Revelation and Understanding.**

And my speech and my preaching were not with persuasive words of human wisdom, but in demonstration of the Spirit and of power, that your faith should not be in the wisdom of men but in the power of God. (2 Corinthians 2:4-5)

These things God has revealed to us through the Spirit. For the Spirit searches all things even the depths of God. Now we have received, not the spirit of the world, but the Spirit who is from God, that we might know the things that have been freely given to us by God. These things we also speak, not in words which man's wisdom teaches but which the Holy Spirit teaches, comparing spiritual things with spiritual. But the natural man does not receive the things of the Spirit of God, for they are foolishness to him; nor can he know them, because they are spiritually discerned. (2 Corinthians 2:10, 12-14).

In *2 Corinthians*, the Holy Spirit is the **Living Guarantee in our hearts** of the promise of Eternal life.

Now He who establishes us with you in Christ and has anointed us is God, who also has sealed us and given us the Spirit in our hearts as a guarantee. (2 Corinthians 1: 22-23).

In ***Galatians,*** the Holy Spirit is our **Fruit Bearer of godly character.**

But the fruit of the Spirit is love, joy, peace, longsuffering, kindness, goodness, faithfulness, gentleness, self-control. Against such there is no law (Galatians 5:22-23)

In ***Ephesians,*** the Holy Spirit is the **Sword of Spiritual warfare.**

And take the helmet of salvation, and the sword of the Spirit, which is the word of God (Ephesians 6: 17).

In ***Philippians,*** the Holy Spirit is the **Spirit of Worship.**

For we are the circumcision, who worship God in the Spirit, rejoice in Christ Jesus, and have no confidence in the flesh. (Philippians 3:3).

In **Colossians,** the Holy Spirit is our **Loved One.**

...who also declared to us your love in the Spirit (Colossians 1:8)

In *1 Thessalonians*, the Holy Spirit is the **Spirit of Holiness** whose operations we must not quench.

For God did not call us to uncleanness, but in holiness. Therefore, he who rejects this does not reject man, but God, who has also given us His Holy Spirit (1 Thessalonians 4:7-8).

Do not quench the Spirit (1 Thessalonians 5:19).

In *2 Thessalonians*, the Holy Spirit is our **Sanctifier for Salvation.**

But we are bound to give thanks to God always for you, brethren beloved by the Lord, because God from the beginning chose you for salvation through sanctification by the Spirit and belief in the truth (2 Thessalonians 2:13).

In *1 Timothy*, the Holy Spirit is the **Speaking Spirit**, warning of Satanic deception, demonic doctrines and deceptive godliness.

Now the Spirit expressly says that in latter times some will depart from the faith, giving heed to deceiving spirits and doctrines of demons (1Timothy 4:1).

In *2 Timothy*, the Holy Spirit is the **Spirit of power, love and a sound mind.**

For God has not given you a spirit of fear, but a Spirit of power, love and a sound mind. (2 Timothy 1:7)

In *Titus*, the Holy Spirit is the **Spirit of Renewal and Restoration.**

Not by works of righteousness which we have done, but according to His mercy He saved us, through the washing of regeneration and renewing of the Holy Spirit (Titus 3:5).

In *Philemon*, the Holy Spirit is the **Spirit of Forgiveness and Reconciliation.**

If then you count me as a partner, receive him as you would me. But if he has wronged you or owes anything, put that on my account. (Philemon 17, 18).

In *Hebrews*, the Holy Spirit is the **Spirit of Grace.**

Of how much worse punishment, do you suppose, will he be thought worthy who has trampled the Son of God underfoot, counted the blood of the covenant by which he was sanctified a common thing, and insulted the Spirit of grace? (Hebrews 10:29).

In *James*, the Holy Spirit is the **Spirit of righteous jealousy.**

Or do you think that the Scripture says in vain, "The Spirit who dwells in us yearns jealously"? (James 4:5).

In *1 Peter*, the Holy Spirit is **Spirit of Glory.**

If you are reproached for the name of Christ, blessed are you, for the Spirit of glory and of God rests upon you. On their part He is blasphemed, but on your part, He is glorified. (1 Peter 4:14).

In *2 Peter*, the Holy Spirit is the **Spirit of Prophecy.**

Knowing this first, that no prophecy of Scripture is of any private interpretation, for prophecy never came by the will of man, but holy men of God spoke as they were moved by the Holy Spirit (1 Peter 1:20-21).

In *1 John*, the Holy Spirit is the **Anointing from the Holy One.**

But you have an anointing from the Holy One, and you know all things. But the anointing which you have received from Him abides in you, and you do not need that anyone teach you; but as the same anointing teaches you concerning all things, and is true, and is not a lie, and just as it has taught you, you will abide in Him. (1 John 2:20, 27).

In *2 John,* the Holy Spirit is the **Spirit of Discernment.**

For many deceivers have gone out into the world who do not confess Jesus Christ as coming in the flesh. This is a deceiver and an antichrist. Look to yourselves, that we do not lose those things we worked for, but that we may receive a full reward (2 John 7-8).

In *3 John,* the Holy Spirit is the **Spirit of Hospitality.**

Beloved, you do faithfully whatever you do for the brethren and for strangers, who have borne witness of your love before the church. If you send them forward on their journey in a manner worthy of God, you will do well. (3 John 5-6).

In *Jude,* the Holy Spirit is the **Spirit of Prayer and our Prayer Partner**

But you, beloved, building yourselves up on your most holy faith, praying in the Holy Spirit. (Jude 20)

In **Revelation**, the Holy Spirit is the **Spirit of Exhortation**

He who has an ear, let him he what the Spirit is saying to the churches. (Revelation 3:6)

CHAPTER 4
REQUIREMENTS TO BE ANOINTED

"How, then, can they call on the one they have not believed in? And how can they believe in the one of whom they have not heard? And how can they hear without someone preaching to them?" (*Romans 10:14*)

To qualify to be an anointed one, a person has to:

1. *Hear the Gospel* as expounded in the following Bible scriptures: John 3:16; Romans 3:21-26; Romans 6:23; Romans 10:4-10; 1 Corinthians 15:1-7; Titus 3:3-7.

A believer in Christ is someone who hears, believes and lives the Gospel of Jesus Christ. What then, is the gospel of our Lord Jesus Christ? Below is an overview of the gospel of salvation:

A. God is holy, loving and just. He therefore, must condemn all sinners to punishment in the flames of eternal hell. Scriptural references include John 3:16 and Romans 6:23.

B. You and I are sinners who deserve nothing but God's wrath; eternal death in hell after earthly death. Scriptural references include Romans 6:23; Romans 8:12-13 and 2 Thessalonians 1:7-10

C. God loves humanity immensely that He sent His Only Son, Jesus (who was fully God and fully man), to die on the cross for our sins. Jesus paid the debt for our sins and absorbed God's wrath on our behalf. Three days later, Jesus resurrected from the dead. Scriptural references include John 3:16; Romans 8:1-4; Ephesians 2:8-9 and 1 Corinthians 15:1-7; 1 Peter 1:17-21.

D. If you repent (acknowledge and turn away) from all your sins, believe that Jesus took your place on the cross, paid your debt of sins and rose from the dead and personally put your faith (Acts 20:21) in Jesus Christ as your Saviour and Lord, you are entitled to eternal life and will receive the GIFT OF THE HOLY SPIRIT (Acts 2:38-39).

2. *Be meek and humble.*

> *Therefore, lay aside all filthiness and overflow of wickedness, and receive with meekness the implanted word, which is able to save your souls. (James 1:21)*

> *For the LORD takes pleasure in His people; He will beautify the humble with salvation. (Psalm 149:4)*

> *For you will save the humble people, but will bring down haughty looks (Psalm 18:27)*

It takes meekness and humility to accept God's way of Salvation. God's way of Salvation is not by righteous works of the law but by the righteousness of faith (Romans 10:1-4) offered through the preaching of the word of faith (Romans 10:5-13).

Jesus humbly loved God's righteousness and hated lawlessness, therefore God anointed Him with the oil of gladness above His fellows (Hebrews 1:8-9). Likewise, when a person hears, believes and accepts God's way of Salvation, He anoints the person with His Spirit.

3. ***Yield to the conviction*** of the Holy Spirit (John 16:7-11) and to godly sorrow (2 Corinthians 7:10) that produces true repentance for you to acknowledge and turn away from your sins.

4. ***Believe the gospel*** as outlined in (1) above involving confessing with your mouth that Jesus is Lord and believing in your heart that God raised Jesus from the dead. (Romans 10:4-6, 9-10).

5. ***In prayer, call on God*** to save you (Romans 10:13).

6. ***Receive Jesus*** and His redemptive, ransom and substitution work on the cross on your behalf (John 1:11-13).

7. ***Get baptised*** in water (Acts 2:38; 1 Peter 3:21).

8. **Have a soul** that thirsts and desires for the Holy Spirit (John 7:37-39; Psalm 42:1-2)

9. *Ask Jesus* to baptize you with the Holy Spirit (Luke 3:16 and Luke11:13).

10.Receive the Holy Spirit (Acts 19:2-7).

If you believe the above with all your heart, pray this prayer below to accept and receive Jesus as your personal Lord and Saviour and to receive the gift of the Holy Spirit:

Dear righteous Lord Jesus, I acknowledge, confess and turn away from my sins. Forgive and cleanse me from my sins, iniquities and transgressions. Oh, my sinless Saviour, you took my place on the cross, paid my debt of sin and tasted eternal death for me. I believe in my heart that God raised you up from the dead on the third day. Give me a new heart and spirit. Anoint, baptize and fill me with your Holy Spirit. Let your love reign in my heart for you and others. Keep me from evil; empower me to be a fruitful and obedient disciple fulfilling your will for my life. Amen.

CHAPTER 5
ANOINTED ONES IN THE BIBLE

When they went from one nation to another, and from one kingdom to another people; Yes, He (God) rebuked kings for their sakes, Saying, do not touch My anointed ones, and do My prophets no harm (1 Chronicles 16:20-22).

There are several persons that were designated as the *Anointed Ones* in the scriptures including:

- The Patriarchs – Abraham, Isaac and Jacob

- The High Priests, Prophets, and Kings of the Old Testament

- Jesus Christ

- New Testament Holy Spirit born believers

The Patriarchs – Abraham, Isaac and Jacob

God referred to the Patriarchs - Abraham, Isaac and Jacob as His Anointed Ones.

The Patriarchs – Abraham, Isaac and Jacob are anointed Prophets. A case in point was when God rebuked the heathen King Abimelech who took Abraham's wife Sarah, when in fear Abraham lied that she was her sister.

Now therefore restore the man his wife; for he is a prophet, and he will pray for you and you will live. But if you do not restore her, know that you shall surely die, you and all who are yours (Genesis 20:7).

As Jacob journeyed back to Bethel in obedience to God's instruction, *the terror of God was upon the cities that were all around them, and they did not pursue the sons of Jacob* (Genesis 35:1,5). God rebuked Laban when he sought to harm Jacob; *Laban said to Jacob, 'it is in my power to do you harm, but the God of your father spoke to me last night, saying, 'Be careful that you speak to Jacob neither good or bad'* (Genesis 31:24, 29).

How comforting and reassuring it is to know that even in our moments of weakness and vulnerability, our God protects us and will not let our enemies harm or destroy us. Thank you, LORD!

Priests, Prophets and Kings

In the old testament priests, prophets and kings that God chose and consecrated for holy purposes and service were referred to as the **Anointed Ones or the LORD'S ANOINTED** (1 Samuel 16:6; 24:6, 10). This is evident in the lives of the High Priest Aaron (Exodus 29:29 and Psalm 133); King Saul, David and Solomon (1 Samuel 9:16; 10:1; 16:12-13; 1 Kings 1:34,39) and Prophets Elisha and Daniel (1 Kings 19:16; Daniel 4:9; 5:11).

By anointing them with holy anointing oil, the Spirit of God came upon them to consecrate and empower them to function in their calling.

And the LORD said, "Arise, anoint him, for this is he". Then Samuel took the horn of oil and anointed him (David) in the midst of his brothers. And the Spirit of the LORD rushed upon David from that day forward (1 Samuel 16:12-13).

When Prophet Samuel anointed David as King, the Spirit of God rushed upon David from that day onwards empowering him to function as the *'Lord's Anointed'*.

But David said to Abishai, "Do not destroy him, for who can put out their hand against the LORD's anointed and be guiltless? As the LORD lives, the LORD will strike him, or his day will come to die, or he will go down into battle and perish. The LORD forbid that I should put out my hand against the LORD's anointed" (1 Samuel 26:9-11)

Before David, Prophet Samuel had anointed Saul as King by God's direction. Even though God later rejected King Saul from reigning because of his disobedience, David acknowledged King Saul as the *'Lord's anointed'* and refused to kill or harm him even when King Saul and his men were after David's life.

The principle here is, as fellow anointed Christians, no matter what the conflict or our grievances, we must

not kill one another in our thoughts, with words or deeds; we must leave vengeance, vindication and judgement for God or we can sow the seeds of mercy when we are wronged as the scripture exhorts, that, *blessed are the merciful for they shall obtain mercy* (Matthew 5:7).

Jesus Christ (the Anointed One)

*How **God anointed Jesus of Nazareth** with the Holy Spirit and with power (Acts 10:38).*

*The Spirit of the LORD GOD is upon me (Jesus) because **He has anointed me** to preach the gospel to the poor (Isaiah 61:1).*

As God's chosen and ultimate Anointed One, Jesus was conceived by the Holy Spirit (Matthew 1:20) and anointed with the Holy Spirit at His baptism (Matthew 3:16). He came in the power of the Spirit (Luke 4:14) from fasting in the wilderness and overcoming temptation. This gave him the strength to preach the gospel (Isaiah 61:1), destroy the works of the devil (1 John 3:8), show signs and wonders (Matthew 12:27-28) and give His life as a ransom for the salvation of sinful men (Mark 10:45 and Acts 4:12).

*Therefore, let all the house of Israel know assuredly that **God has made Jesus**, whom you crucified, **both Lord and Christ** (the **Anointed One**). (Acts 2:36).*

*For there is salvation in **no one else**, for there is **no other name except Jesus** under heaven given among men by which we may be saved. (Acts 4:12).*

God chose and designated Jesus as His Anointed One (Messiah or Christ).

Holy Spirit Born Believers

*That which is **born of the flesh is flesh, and that which is born of the Spirit is spirit.** Do not marvel that I said to you, you must be born again. (John 3:6-7)*

*But to all who did receive Him (Jesus) who believed in His Name, He gave the right to become children of God, **who were born, not of blood nor of the will of the flesh nor of the will of man, but of God** (John 1:12)*

In the New Testament, one becomes a believer when he hears, believe and receives the Gospel message (1 Corinthians 15:1-7; Romans 10:4-10). That is, the person has believed and received Christ (John 1:12). The believer is said to be born again (John 3:3-7). The believer must also undergo water baptism as an outward sign of the inward regenerated work of the Holy Spirit signifying his identification with the death, burial and resurrection of Christ through the waters of baptism (Mark 16:15-16; 1 Peter 3:21; Titus 3:3-7).

*Now He who now establishes us with you in Christ **and has anointed us is God, who has also sealed us and given us the Spirit in our hearts** as a guarantee* (2 Corinthians 1:21-22).

The believer has to be baptized with the Holy Spirit (Luke 3:16; Acts 2:38; 2 Corinthians 1:21) by the Holy Spirit's falling (Acts 10:44-46) on him or having the Holy Spirit imparted through the laying on of hands (Acts 8:14-20; Acts 19:1-7) by anointed leaders gifted with that grace.

It is one thing to be born of the Spirit (John 3:6-7; John 20:20-22; Acts 8:14-16; Acts 19:1-7) and it is another thing to be baptized or anointed with the Holy Spirit (Luke 3:16; Acts 1:8).

All Believers who have been baptized or anointed with the Holy Spirit by Jesus Christ (Luke 3:16) are called Anointed Ones (1 John 2:20).

*But you have been **anointed** by the **Holy One** (**Mark 1:24**) and you all have knowledge (1 John 2:20)*

*There is One coming after me (John the Baptist), whose sandals I am not worthy to remove. **He (Jesus Christ) shall baptize you with the Holy Spirit** and with fire (power) (Luke 3:16).*

Anointed Ones are Spirit-born and Spirit-baptized believers.

The Holy Spirit's baptism is the gateway or initiation into the anointing.

And do not get drunk with wine, for that is debauchery, but be filled with the Spirit (Ephesians 5:18)

Being filled continually with the Holy Spirit empowers the believer into greater depths for supernatural works and the manifestation of God's nature and life through him.

*On the last day of the feast, Jesus stood up and cried out, "if anyone thirsts; let him come to me and drink. Whoever believes in me, as the Scripture has said, **out of his heart will flow rivers of living water". Now this he said about the Spirit, whom those who believed in Him were to receive.** (John 7:37-39)*

That is why the Bible commands believers to be continuously filled with the Holy Spirit even after the initial baptism of the Holy Spirit.

This is also illustrated in the **vision of Ezekiel in Ezekiel 47** where the *'water of the Spirit'* issuing from the altar of the Temple started as a trickle from the south side of the Temple and gradually went ankle-deep to knee-deep to waist deep and became a big river that produced fresh fishes and fruitful trees. That is what happens with life in the Holy Spirit.

It starts with a **'trickle'** conviction of the Holy Spirit (John 16:7-8) in our heart with godly sorrow to acknowledge, confess and forsake our sinful life and embrace the need for Jesus as our personal Saviour.

At '**ankle-deep**' the Spirit helps us respond to the Gospel message and we call on Jesus to forgive our sins and save us (Romans 10:8-13).

At '**knee-deep**' we are 'born again', not of perishable seed but imperishable, through the living and abiding word of God (1 Peter 1:23). At 'knee-deep' the Holy Spirit initiates new birth (John 3:6-7), new life (John 6:63), and imparts divine nature (Ephesians 4:24; 2 Peter 1:4) to the person who has confessed and received Christ.

At '**waist-deep**' the Holy Spirit nudges us to seek water baptism and Spirit baptism. The water baptism makes a public and spiritual declaration to angels, humans and demons that we have identified with the death, burial and resurrection of Christ and have been translated from the Kingdom of darkness to the Kingdom of light. And the Holy Spirit baptism initiates the believer into the anointing and power of God. At 'waist-deep' the **believer is in union with Christ and is an Anointed one.** Christ is formed in the believer and he is growing in the grace and knowledge of our Lord Jesus Christ (Galatians 4:19; 2 Peter 3:18).

At the **'living river'** level, the believer is full and overflowing with the power (gifts) and nature (fruit) of the Holy Spirit (1 Corinthians 12:1-11; Galatians 5:22-26). The 'living river' believer is not a novice in Christ but a mature son or daughter of Christ who is led by the Holy Spirit, winning others to Christ and fulfilling the calling and ministry he has received from the Lord (Colossians 4:17; Romans 12:3-8; Ephesians 4:7-11) and excelling in it.

Power Truths

1. Jesus is the Christ – the ultimate Anointed One

2. In the Old Testament – Patriarchs, Prophets, Priests and Kings who were consecrated for God's service with the holy anointing oil were called the LORD's Anointed or Anointed Ones.

3. In the New Testament, persons who have heard and sincerely believed the Gospel of Christ (1 Corinthians 15:1-7) and are born and baptized by the Holy Spirit (John 3:3-7; Luke 3:16) are called Anointed Ones.

4. Anointed Ones are people who receive the Holy Spirit when they believe in Jesus Christ. (Acts 19:1-7).

5. Anointed Ones are people who have the Holy Spirit of God in them. *For anyone who does not have the Spirit of God does not belong to Christ* (Romans 8:9; Jude 19).

CHAPTER 6
THE ULTIMATE ANOINTED ONE

The 'Anointed One' in the Old Testament

And He (Jesus) was handed a book of the Prophet Isaiah. And when He had opened the book, He found the place where it was written: "The Spirit of the LORD is upon me for **He has anointed me (Jesus)** *to preach the Gospel to the poor; he has sent me to heal the broken hearted, to proclaim liberty to the captives, and recovery of sight to the blind, to set at liberty those who are oppressed; to proclaim the acceptable year of the LORD"*

Then he closed the book and gave it back to the attendant and sat down. And the eyes of all who were in the synagogue were fixed on Him, and He began to say, "Today this Scripture is fulfilled in your hearing" (Luke 4:17-21)

Jesus the Christ (Anointed One)

Yeshua ha-Mashiach is Hebrew for Jesus the Messiah or Jesus the Anointed One. *Mashiach* is derived from the verb *Mashach* which means 'to anoint' by applying the holy anointing oil to a person.

In the Old Testament the word anointed was originally used to refer to Priests, Prophets and Kings that God chose and consecrated for holy purposes and service.

The Prophets of the Old Testament also used the word Messiah or Anointed One to refer to the coming of the chosen **Prince** (Isaiah 9:6-7; Daniel 9:25-26), the **Prophet** (Deuteronomy 18:15, 18), the **King** (Zechariah 9:9; Matthew 2:1-2; John 18:37-39) and the **Saviour** (Acts 5:30-31; Luke 1:68-75) who will complete the redemption purpose of God to redeem mankind from sin and eternal death. This was fulfilled in Jesus who is the chief or ultimate Anointed One (John 4:25-26; Luke 4:16-21 and Acts 1:38).

The Messiah – **ruler over earthly kings** (Revelation 1:5), the great **High Priest after the order of Melchizedek** (Hebrews 5:6) and **Saviour** who saves humanity from sin and dominion of the devil (1 John 3:8) by His sacrificial and substitutionary death on the cross.

The 'Anointed One' in the Gospels

He said to them, "but who do you say that I am?" Simon Peter replied, **"you are the Christ (the Anointed One, the Messiah),** *the Son of the Living God". And Jesus answered him, "blessed are you, Simon Bar-Jonah! For flesh and blood has not revealed this to you, but My Father who is in heaven". Then He commanded His disciples that* **they should tell no one that He was Jesus the Christ.** *(Matthew 16:15-17, 20).*

In the New Testament the word **'Messiah'** is **'Christos'** in *Greek*, or **'Christ'** in *English* which is translated as **Anointed One.**

> **Christ is not the surname of Jesus; it is His title. Jesus Christ therefore means Jesus the Anointed One.**

In the Gospels, Jesus never denied that He wasn't the Anointed One (Messiah) rather He confirmed it in John 4:25,

29 and Matthew 27:11. People believed Jesus is the Messiah – the Christ (John 1:40-41; 9:35-38 and Luke 9:20), the ultimate Anointed One sent from God as:

- The Prophet like unto Moses (Deuteronomy 28:15, 18; Acts 3:17-26; Acts 7: 35-39).

- Emmanuel – God with us (Isaiah 7:14; Matthew 1:23).

- Wonderful, Counsellor (Isaiah 9:6; Judges 13:18).

- Mighty God, Everlasting Father (Isaiah 9:6; Titus 2:13).

- The Prince of Peace (Isaiah 9:6; Ephesians 2:14).

- Saviour (Luke 2:11).

- Redeemer (1 Corinthians 1:30; Isaiah 59:20).

- Son of David concerning His human descent (Romans 1:3-4; Luke 1:32-33; Luke 18:38; Matthew 12:23-28; Matthew 20:30-34; Matthew 21:9-16 and Matthew 22:41-46).

- Son of God concerning His divinity (Matthew 16:13-17; Matthew 22:41-46; Luke 1:34-35; Luke 20:41-44 and Romans 1:3-4).

- King of the Jews (Matthew 2:2; Matthew 27:11, 29, 37).

- The Ruler over the kings on the earth (Revelation 1:5).

He (Andrew) first found his own brother Simon and said we have found **the Messiah which is translated, the Christ** *(the Anointed One). And he brought him to Jesus (John 1:41-42).*

The woman said to him, **"I know that Messiah is coming, who is called Christ** *(the Anointed One). When He comes, He will tell us all things". Jesus said to her, "I who speak to you am He". (John 4:25-26).* **Jesus told the Samaritan woman He is the Messiah, the Anointed One.**

The Jews and religious leaders of His day refused to acknowledge or accept Jesus' assertion that He is the Christ, the Anointed One. As a matter of fact, it was the reason why they condemned Him to death by crucifixion. Till today, orthodox Jews still reject Jesus as the Messiah, the Anointed One (Christ).

His claim that He is the Anointed King infuriated them, but they could not disprove His assertion. **He is the Son of David by His human descent and the Son of God by divine descent; the ultimate Anointed King who is greater than David and Abraham,** *for even before Abraham was, Jesus said "I am". (John 8:52-58 and Revelation 1:8).*

The 'Anointed One' in the Book of Acts

In the Book of Acts, **the apostles contended and defended the truth that Jesus is the Christ – the Anointed One.** Peter, Stephen, Apollos and Paul all contended for this truth.

Then Paul as was his custom went in to them and for three Sabbaths reasoned with them from the Scriptures, explaining and demonstrating that Christ had to suffer and rise again from the dead saying, **"this Jesus whom I preach to you is the Christ (the Anointed One).** *(Acts 17:3).*

Apostle Paul

*Therefore, let all the house of Israel know assuredly that **God has made Jesus**, whom you crucified, **both Lord and Christ (Anointed One)**. (Acts 2:36).*

Apostle Peter

*They departed from the presence of the council, rejoicing that they were counted worthy to suffer shame for His name. And daily in the temple, and in every house, they did not cease teaching and preaching **Jesus as the Christ (Anointed One)**. (Acts 5:41-42).*

Apostles of Jesus

*"You stiff-necked and uncircumcised in heart and ears! You always resist the Holy Spirit; as your fathers did, so do you. Which of the prophets did your fathers not persecute? And they killed those who foretold the coming of the Just One (**the Christ - the Anointed One**) of whom you now have become betrayers and murderers"* (Acts 7:51-52)

Deacon Stephen

*When Silas and Timothy had come from Macedonia, **Paul was compelled by the Spirit, and testified to the Jews that***

Jesus is the Christ (the Anointed One, the Messiah). But when they opposed him and blasphemed, he shook his garments and said to them; "your blood be upon your own heads; I am clean. From now on I will go to the Gentiles" (Acts 18:5-6).

Apostle Paul

*He greatly helped those who believed through grace, for He vigorously refuted the Jews publicly, showing from the scriptures that **Jesus is the Christ (the Anointed One)** (Acts 18:27-28).*

Teacher Apollos

From the above Scriptures, the truth that ***Jesus is the Christ*** (the ***Anointed One***) is the teaching of Jesus and the apostles.

*For many **deceivers** have gone out into the world who **don't confess Jesus Christ (the Anointed One) as coming in the flesh.** This is deceptive. Whoever transgresses and does not abide in the doctrine of Christ does not have God. He who abides in the doctrine of Christ has both the Father and the Son. **If anyone comes to you and does not have this doctrine, do not receive him into your house nor greet him** (2 John 1:7, 9-10).*

*In their case the god of this world has **blinded the minds of unbelievers**, keeping them from seeing the light of the gospel of the glory of Christ, who is the image of God. For what **we proclaim is not ourselves but Jesus Christ as Lord** with ourselves as servants for Jesus' sake (2 Corinthians 4:4-5).*

*And the Lord's servant must not be quarrelsome but kind to everyone, able to teach, patiently enduring evil, correcting opponents with gentleness. God may perhaps grant them **repentance leading to the knowledge of the truth** and they may come to their senses and escape from the snare of the devil, after being captured by him to do His will (2 Timothy 2:24-26).*

According to the Bible any preacher, prophet, apostle, bishop, teacher, religion, institution or persons who deny Jesus is the Anointed One, who came in the flesh for the purpose of sinful humanity's redemption, is influenced by the spirit of the Anti-Christ. We are admonished not to welcome their erroneous teaching but rather pray for them that by revelation and knowledge they will repent and come to the knowledge of the truth that Jesus is the Messiah, the Christ (the Anointed One).

Power Truths

- Christ is not the surname of Jesus. It means Messiah or Anointed One. *Yeshua ha-Mashiach* means Jesus the Messiah – the Christ.

- In the Old Testament, Prophets, Priests and Kings were anointed with Holy anointing oil (a symbol of the Holy Spirit), consecrating them for God's service.

- God anointed Jesus with the Holy Spirit for His Incarnation (Matthew 1:20), sinless life (Hebrews 4:14-15 and Hebrews 9:14), divine commission (Isaiah 61:1-3), good works (Acts 10:38), death (Hebrews 9:14) and resurrection (Romans 1:2-4) for sinful humanity's redemption.

- God made Jesus who was crucified both Lord and Christ (the *Anointed One, Messiah*) by raising him from the dead. (Acts 2:29-36 and Romans 1:3-4).

- As God's Anointed One, Jesus is the Apostle, Prophet, King, Saviour and High Priest (Hebrews 3:1-2) of a new and better Covenant.

- Jesus, the Anointed One is the Son of David after His human descent and is the Son of God after His divine descent. (Luke 1:34-35; Romans 1:3-4; Acts 2:22-36; Matthew 22:41-46).

- Jesus grants forgiveness of sins and eternal life to all who believe in Him and anoints them with the Holy Spirit. (Luke 3:16 Acts 2:29-33, 38-39).

- The doctrine of Christ and the apostolic teaching is that Jesus is the Christ (the Messiah, the Anointed One). According to the Bible, persons and institutions who deny this are operating under the influence of the spirit of the Anti-Christ. True Christians are admonished not to fellowship with them (2 John 1:7, 9-10). We are to pray for such people to comprehend and apprehend the divine revelation and foundational truth that Jesus is the Anointed One (Matthew 16:14-18; 2 Timothy 2:24-26; 1 Peter 3:15 and 2 Corinthians 4:3-6).

CHAPTER 7
THE BAPTIZER AND ANOINTER

"I (John) baptize you with water for repentance, but He (Christ) who is coming after me is mightier than I, whose sandals I am not worthy to carry. He will baptize you with the Holy Spirit and fire" (Matthew 3:11).

As the ultimate Anointed One, the Messiah - the CHRIST, He has a more excellent name than the Patriarchs, the Prophets and Angels. For the purpose of humanity's redemption and to destroy the devil's work of sin, sickness, curses, poverty and death, God anointed Jesus with the Holy Spirit and power.

God anointed Jesus of Nazareth with the Holy Spirit and power as He went about doing good and healing all that were oppressed by the devil because God was with him (Acts 10:38)

"The Spirit of the Lord is upon me for He has anointed me to bring good news to the poor; He has sent me to bind up the broken hearted, to proclaim liberty to the captives, the opening of prison to those who are bound; to proclaim the year of the Lord's favour and the day of vengeance of our God, to comfort all who mourn" (Isaiah 61:1-2).

If Jesus needed to be anointed for His divine purpose and commission, then we too have to be anointed. Being Spirit-born is not enough. We need to be Spirit-baptized. **John is not the only Baptist; Jesus is a Baptist too.** Listen to John the Baptist testifying that **Jesus is a Baptist not with water, but with the Holy Spirit:**

I (John) baptize you with water for repentance, but He (Christ) who is coming after me is mightier than I, whose sandals I am not worthy to carry. He will baptize you with the Holy Spirit and fire (Matthew 3:11)

Remember Jesus was conceived by the Holy Spirit and was anointed with the Holy Spirit at His water baptism; when John the Baptist baptized Him in the Jordan River something amazing happened:

*"The heavens were opened, and **the Holy Spirit descended on Him like a dove** and a voice from heaven said, this is my beloved Son in whom I am well pleased, listen to Him (Luke 3:21-22).*

God sent Jesus into the world to save sinners. Jesus sent believers to preach the Gospel to the lost world and make disciples of all nations.

God anointed Jesus with the Holy Spirit and Jesus baptized those who believed in Him.

*On the last day of the feast, Jesus stood up and cried out with a loud voice: "If anyone thirsts, let him come and drink. Whoever believes in me as the scripture has said, out of his heart will flow rivers of living water". **Now He said this to those who believed in Him and were to receive Christ and His** Spirit. For the Spirit had not been given because Jesus was not yet glorified (John 7:37-39).*

When Jesus was glorified by the resurrection from the dead by the Spirit of Holiness, and declared Lord and Christ, He baptized the apostles and disciples who believed with Holy Spirit in the upper room (Acts 1:8).

Jesus is ready to baptize anyone who believes in Him for salvation with the Holy Spirit.

No wonder the Apostle Paul asked the Ephesians: **"did you receive the Holy Spirit when you believed?" (Acts 19:1-7).** Anyone who has believed the Gospel (1 Corinthians 15:1-7) and confessed Christ Jesus (Romans 10:9-10) should have the Holy Spirit fall on him (Acts 10:44-48) or hands laid on him by a Spirit-filled Christian leader that is graced with the ability to impart the gift of the Holy Spirit. (Acts 8:14-20).

Sadly, the Ephesians said they didn't hear of the Holy Spirit. Apostle Paul asked them: **"into what baptism then were you baptized?"** They said John's baptism.

John's baptism is with water, but Jesus' baptism is with the Holy Spirit.

*If you then being evil know how to give good gifts to your children, how much more will **God give the Holy Spirit to those who ask Him?** (Luke 11:13).*

New believers have to <u>ask</u> Jesus to baptize them with the Holy Spirit.

*But you have been **anointed by the Holy One** (Jesus Christ) and you have knowledge (1 John 2:20). Jesus Christ is the **Holy One** of God (Mark 1:24).*

If you are baptized with the Holy Spirit, then you are anointed, you are an Anointed One!

As an anointed one, there are attitudes you have to manifest, responsibilities you have to discharge, privileges and blessings you have to enjoy. We will explore these in the coming chapters of 8 - 11.

Power Truths

1. God anointed Jesus Christ with the Holy Spirit at His water baptism.

2. John the Baptist's baptism was only water baptism, not Holy Spirit baptism.

3. There are some believers in Christ who are water baptized but not Spirit baptized (Acts 8:14-1 and Acts 19:1-6).

4. Jesus is the baptizer. Jesus baptizes those who believe in Him for salvation with the Holy Spirit (Luke 3:16; John 7:37-39).

5. All Believers who are baptized with the Holy Spirit by Jesus Christ can be called Anointed Ones (1 John 2:20).

6. All truly Spirit-born and Spirit-baptized believers in Christ are Anointed ones.

7. Anointed Ones have attitudes to manifest, responsibilities to discharge, privileges and blessings to enjoy.

8. Have you believed the Gospel of Christ? Are you born of the Holy Spirit? Have you been baptized with the Holy Spirit? Are you an anointed one?

CHAPTER 8
ATTITUDES OF ANOINTED ONES

"Ability is what you are capable of doing. Motivation determines what you do. Attitude determines how well you do it".

Lou Holtz

Anointed ones have these attitudes towards God, others and themselves:

1. **Contrite heart**

   They are quick to admit, repent and forsake their sins when they sin or make a mistake. (Leviticus 4:1-3; Psalm 51; Psalm 32:5; 38:18 and 1 John 1:5-10)

2. Humility

They do not think of themselves more highly than they ought to, they think of themselves soberly. They are unselfish. They submit themselves to the Word, Will and Ways of God. (Philippians 2:3-11)

3. Brave

They are not cowards as seen in the lives of David, Joshua, Caleb, Shadrach, Meshach and Abednego (Daniel 3; 1 Samuel 17 and Numbers 13:30). Peter denied Christ before a servant girl (Matthew 26:69-75) but after being anointed with the Holy Spirit he was brave; when persecuted and threatened with death by the Sanhedrin group to stop preaching about Christ. He boldly declared that he will rather obey God than men. (Acts 5:27-33).

4. Love what God loves and hates what God hates

Anointed Ones are Lovers of righteousness and haters of iniquity (Hebrews 1:9; Psalm 18:20; Job 29:14; 1 John 2:29; 3:7).

5. **Givers**

Abraham gave tithes by revelation not compulsion. They do not neglect the house of God, its service and the ministers of God (Nehemiah 10:32-39; Malachi 3:8; Hebrews 7:1-9; Genesis 28:22; Deuteronomy 12:1-7, 19). They do not appear before God empty handed. David said, *"I will not give to God anything that will not cost me"*. They make vows and fulfil them (Malachi 1:14; Psalm 116:18; Psalm 66:13; Hosea 14:2; Isaiah 19:19-22).

6. **Enquire of the Lord**

Seeking God's divine direction and help; not leaning on their own wisdom and understanding. As exemplified in the life of David (Psalm 27:4).

7. **Forgivers**

As exemplified in the life of Joseph and Stephen. Joseph forgave his brothers who mistreated him. Stephen, the first Christian martyr forgave those who stoned him to death. (Acts 7:59)

8. **Endurance**

They patiently endure and overcome temptation, tests and trials of their Faith. They run with perseverance the Christian race set before them looking unto Jesus. They learn obedience through God's discipline and suffering according to the will of God (1 Peter 4:12-16; 2 Timothy 2:3; Hebrews 5:8 and Hebrews 12:1-2).

9. **Faith Walkers**

They walk by faith and not by sight (Hebrews 11 and 2 Corinthians 5:7), like Noah who by faith when warned of things as yet unseen, in reverent fear built an ark for the saving of his family (Hebrews 11:7).

10. **Leadership**

They have the spirit of leadership. They are trailblazers and pioneer new moves of God. They are role models and unafraid of unchartered territories. They follow God and lead others to follow Him. Examples include Abraham (Genesis 18:19) and Paul (Philippians 4:9 and 2 Timothy 2:2)

CHAPTER 9
RESPONSIBILITIES OF ANOINTED ONES

When I was a child, I spoke like a child, I thought like a child. When I became a man, I gave up childish ways.

1 Corinthians 13:11

"A people that value its privileges above its" principles soon lose both.

Dwight D Eisenhower

Here are ten responsibilities of Anointed sons and daughters:

1. **Be Spirit led**

    To be led by the Holy Spirit (Romans 8:14).

2. **Be an ardent student of the Word of God**

    Read, memorize, study, meditate and rightly divide the word of truth (2 Timothy 2:15).

3. **Be a God pleaser**

    Discern God's will and do what pleases Him (Ephesians 5:10; and Hebrews 5:14).

4. **Be a lover of truth**

    Love the truth and walk in the truth (2 John1:4 and Romans 1:18, 25).

5. **Be submitted to divine and delegated authority**

    Do not undermine or usurp divine and delegated authority. Submit to divine order and authority (1 Peter 2:17 and Jude 8-11).

6. **Do not be covetous**

Do not merchandise your gifts; freely you have received, freely give (2 Corinthians 4:1-2 and 1Timothy 6:5-10).

7. **Be a person of integrity**

Manifest godly character and integrity (Titus 1:6-9).

8. **Be a Worshipper**

Give thanks to God always, praise and worship Him (Colossians 3:16 and Ephesians 5:18-19).

9. **Be a minister of the Spirit**

... our sufficiency is of God, who also made us sufficient as **ministers of the new covenant, not of the letter but of the Spirit**; *for the letter kills, but the Spirit gives life* (2 Cor 3:5-6).

They minister and impart the Spirit.

10. **Be undefiled, maintaining spiritual health and fitness**

They engage the disciplines of fasting and prayer. They maintain spiritual hygiene and cleanliness. They take responsibility to keep their spirit, soul and body pure. (2 Corinthians 7:1;1 Timothy 5:22; Ecclesiastes 19:8 and Isaiah 52:11; Isaiah 58).

CHAPTER 10
PRIVILEGES OF ANOINTED ONES

"What separates privilege from entitlement is gratitude".

Brene Brown

Anointed ones have the listed privileges:

1. Anointed Ones receive **divine dreams and visions** from the Spirit of God (Joel 2: 28).

2. Anointed sons and daughters **prophesy** (Joel 2:28) as they are commanded, and **miraculous** results happens (Ezekiel 37).

3. They **manifest the gifts of the Holy Spirit** for the profit of all (1 Corinthians 12:7).

4. They have the **support and favour of men** to fulfil their divine destiny (2 Samuel :4-7; 1 Chronicles 12:18)

5. Those who despise them come under **God's judgment and disfavour or rebuke.** (1 Samuel 25:10; Numbers 12:10)

6. They have **favour with God** (Romans 9:13; Luke 1:30; Luke 2:52).

7. God blesses those who **bless them and curses those who curse** them (Genesis 12:3; Numbers 23:7-8, 18-23)

8. *God tells them His secrets* (Psalm 25:14; Genesis 18:17-18).

9. **The grace of longevity.** Moses an anointed man under the old testament was 120 years; his eyes were not dim, nor his strength abated. (Deuteronomy 34:7; Isaiah 65:20).

10. Anointed ones experience **miraculous provision, protection and authority.** Peter escaped Herod's

sword. Joshua commanded the sun to stand still; Hezekiah had a sign of shadow moving back ten degrees. Angels stopped the mouth of the lions to protect Daniel. The bones of Elisha raised the dead. Handkerchiefs of Paul healed and casted out demons. Samson carried the gates of the city up on the mountain. Peter witnessed the prison gates opened by itself; Paul was bitten by a venomous snake and he shakes it off and suffers no harm. Elijah outran the chariots of Ahab, Philip appears in Azotos by divine flight. The Red Sea parted, Jesus walked on the sea and multiplied small food. As an Anointed one believe for and expect miracles from the Spirit of God.

CHAPTER 11
BLESSINGS OF ANOINTED ONES

The blessing of the Lord makes rich and He adds no sorrow with it.

Proverbs 10:22

God blesses those He has anointed. God also makes them a blessing to others. This is clearly seen in the lives of Abraham and Joseph. Abraham refused to take the spoils of war from the King of Sodom lest he says he made Abraham rich (Genesis 14:22-23).

Abraham attributed his wealth and riches to the Lord Most High. He believed that God did not only bless him but made him a blessing to other people so that in him all the families of the earth shall be blessed (Genesis 12:3). Joseph was a blessing to Potiphar's house, his wicked brothers and to the whole nation of Egypt (Genesis 39:1-6). As an anointed one, you are blessed and a blessing to many. Let us look at some of these blessings in further detail:

1. The blessing of divine protection

You are untouchable by demons. Those who plot and conspire against you shall be destroyed by their own evil plots and schemes. Haman was hanged in his own gallows that he prepared for Mordecai, an Anointed one in the book of Esther 7:10. God sent his angels to shut the mouth of the lions when the enemies of Daniel conspired to get him thrown in the lion's den; but they were eaten by the lions when they were thrown in the lion's den. (1 Chronicles 16:22; Psalm 105:15; Luke 10:19. Daniel 3)

2. The generational blessing

They have generational blessings. (Exodus 40:12-15; Exodus 3:3-6; 20:5-6)

3. The blessing of mighty children

Their children are mighty in the earth (2 Samuel 22:51)

4. The blessing of long life

Anointed ones do not die pre-maturely; God satisfies them with long life. (Psalm 91)

5. They live in divine health

They enjoy divine healing from sicknesses; they experience sound health and a good old age. (Genesis 15:15)

6. They are fruitful and increase

No barrenness, only fruitfulness, multiplication and increase. For example, with Isaac, he increased, multiplied and wax great until he was the envy of his neighbours (Genesis 26:12-14).

7. They are planted in the house of God

They flourish and are fruitful in their seasons (Psalm 1; Psalm 92:12-13)

8. The commanded blessing of God is on all they do and have.

It comes to those who are upright in the Lord. (Deuteronomy 28:8; Proverbs 10:22; Mark 10:30)

9. The Blessing of fame and greatness

God makes them famous and their names great. Their names, memory and works live on after their death. (Genesis 12:2; Joshua 6:27; Deuteronomy 26:18-19; Matthew 14:1; Mark 1:28)

10. They are a blessing to their communities, nations and the world

Anointed ones are not only blessed but a blessing to their families, communities and nations. The disciples were anointed with the Holy Spirit to be witnesses for Christ in Jerusalem, Judea, and Samaria and the outermost parts of the earth. **As an anointed one you are destined for global impact.** (Genesis 12:1-3; Acts 1:8)

CHAPTER 12
MY CLOSING THOUGHTS

I trust that the knowledge and illuminations in this book has been a great blessing to you. When you are anointed with the Holy Spirit, you are not a mere person. You are empowered to live a supernatural life.

I will use the parts of the body to illustrate how being anointed empowers us to exert Godly influence:

1. Your **anointed head** will overflow with **wisdom and blessings** from God.

*You **anoint my head** with oil; My cup runs over* (Psalm 23:5).

*It is the **precious oil upon the head** of Aaron, for there the Lord commanded the blessing – life forevermore* (Psalm 133:1-3).

*I have heard of you [Daniel], that the **Spirit of God** is in you, and that **light, understanding and excellent wisdom** are found in you* (Daniel 5:4).

2. Your **anointed eyes** will see into the **spirit realm to avoid spiritual blindness and pitfalls.**

Anoint your eyes** with eye salve that you may **see (Rev 3:18).

*Leave them alone. They are blind leaders of the blind. If the **blind leads the blind, both will fall into a ditch*** (Matthew 15:14).

3. Your **anointed ears** will hear the voice and words of God and be guided by them.

*Your **ears shall hear a word** behind you saying, "this is the way, walk in it"* (Isaiah 30:21).

4. Your **anointed lips** will utter the knowledge of God, not wickedness or deceit.

*My words come from my upright heart; **my lips** utter pure knowledge* (Job 33:3).

My lips will not speak wickedness, nor my tongue utter *deceit* (Job 27:4).

5. Your **anointed tongue** shall utter **kind, just and healing words**; it will not be a **world of iniquity**.

*A **wholesome tongue is a tree of life** but perverseness breaks the spirit* (Proverbs 15:4)

*And his tongue talks of **justice*** (Psalm 37:30)

*And the **tongue is a fire, a world of iniquity**. The tongue is set among our members that it defiles the whole body and sets on fire the course of nature; it is set on fire by hell* (James 3:6)

6. Your **anointed mouth** will speak **Godly wisdom**.

The mouth of the ***righteous speaks wisdom*** and his tongue talks of justice (Psalm 37:30)

For I will give you a ***mouth and wisdom*** which all your adversaries will not be able to contradict or resist. (Luke 21:15)

7. Your **anointed face will radiate hope**.

And fixing his eyes on him, with John, Peter said, *"Look at us."* So, he gave them his attention, expecting to receive something from them. Then Peter said, *"silver and gold I do not have, but what I do have I give to you: In the name of Jesus Christ of Nazareth, rise up and walk."* *(Acts 3:4-6)*

8. Your **anointed hear**t will **love and understand God**.

Now hope does not disappoint because the *love of God has been poured out in our hearts by the Holy Spirit* who was given to us (Romans 5:5)

9. Your **anointed hands** will **heal the sick and impart the Holy Spirit.**

They will *lay hands* on the sick and they will *recover* (Mark 16:18)

And when Simon saw that through the *laying on of the apostles' hands the Holy Spirit was given*, he offered them money, saying, "give me this power also, that anyone on whom I lay hands may receive the Holy Spirit." (Acts 8:18-19)

Now *God worked unusual miracles by the hands of Paul,* so that handkerchiefs were brought from his body to the sick, and the diseases left them, and the evil spirits went out of them (Acts 19:11-12)

And Ananias went his way and entered the house; and *laying his hands on him* he said, "Brother Saul, the Lord Jesus, who appeared to you on the road as you came, has sent me that you may receive your sight and be filled with the Holy Spirit." (Acts 9:17)

10. Your **anointed feet** will go to the **nations preaching the gospel.**

And having *shod your feet* with the preparation of the *Gospel of peace* (Ephesians 6:15)

How *beautiful upon the mountains are the feet of him who brings good news,* who proclaims peace, who brings glad tidings of good things, who proclaims salvation, who says to Zion, "Your God reigns!" (Isaiah 52:7)

Live the anointed life, be strong in the Lord, do exploits, turn our generation from darkness to light, from doubt to faith in Christ and more importantly, from a non-anointed life to an anointed life. God richly bless you!

<u>Contact the Author</u>

Facebook: Raphael Samuels

Facebook Page: Convicting hearts

YouTube: Rev Raphael Samuels

Instagram: raphael_reigns45

Instagram: Convictinghearts

Website: www.convictinghearts.com

Email: pastorraph45@gmail.com

Blog: www.convictinghearts.wordpress.com

Twitter: convictinghearts

Church website: www.rgci.net

<u>NOTES</u>

www.ingramcontent.com/pod-product-compliance
Lightning Source LLC
Chambersburg PA
CBHW060959050726
47592CB00003B/1266